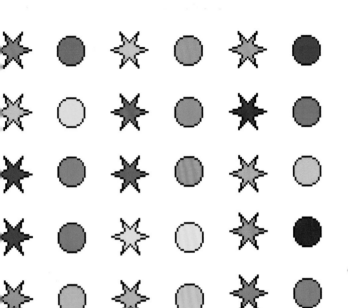

YES! **NO**

IT'S A TIE!

IF YOU CAN TOUCH YOUR FINGER TO YOUR NOSE WITH YOUR EYES SHUT, GO FORWARD 2 SPACES.

CHASED BY EVIL SPACE MONKEYS! GO BACK TO THE START.

PLAY ROCK, PAPER, SCISSORS. LOSER GOES BACK 1 SPACE.

YOU DROPPED YOUR CAKE IN A PUDDLE. GO BACK TO THE LAST GREEN SPACE.

TELL A JOKE. IF SOMEONE LAUGHS GO FORWARD 2 SPACES.

YOU LOSE STAMPY'S LOVELY BOOK. GO BACK TO THE LAST ORANGE SPACE.

MISS A TURN AS YOU WAIT FOR YOUR SPACE PIZZA TO BE DELIVERED.

YOU BUMP INTO SQUID WHILE ON A SPACE WALK. MISS A TURN WHILE YOU HAVE A CHAT.

PULL SOME SILLY FACES FOR YOUR FRIENDS AND THEN GO FORWARD 1 SPACE.

DO YOUR BEST IMPRESSION OF STAMPY CAT. MOVE FORWARD 2 SPACES.

OH DEAR! YOU TRIP OVER. BUT NEVER MIND. IT MOVES YOU FORWARD TO THE NEXT RED SPACE.

YOU PUT ON ODD SOCKS THIS MORNING. MOVE QUICKLY FORWARD 2 SPACES SO NOBODY NOTICES!

SQAISHEY MAKES YOU A LOVELY CHOCOLATE CAKE. MISS A TURN WHILE YOU TUCK IN.

YOU HAVE A GAME OF CHASE WITH BARNABY. MOVE FORWARD 1 SPACE.

YOU GET STUCK BEHIND A SLOW ROCKET. GO BACK 2 SPACES AS YOU FLY ROUND THEM.

YOU PUT THE WRONG ROCKET FUEL IN YOUR SHIP THIS MORNING. GO BACK 1 SPACE.

YOU GO ON A SECRET SPACE MISSION WITH AMY LEE. MOVE TO THE NEXT BLUE SPACE.

THE GRAVITY MACHINE GOES WRONG. BUT NEVER MIND. YOU FLOAT FORWARD 2 SPACES.

THE CAKE IS NEARLY ALL GONE! PRESS OVERDRIVE TO FIND SOME MORE. GO FORWARD 2 SPACES.

YOU FIND LUNA HAS STOWED AWAY. MOVE FORWARD 1 SPACE TO CELEBRATE.

STICK WITH STAMPY!
STICKER BOOK

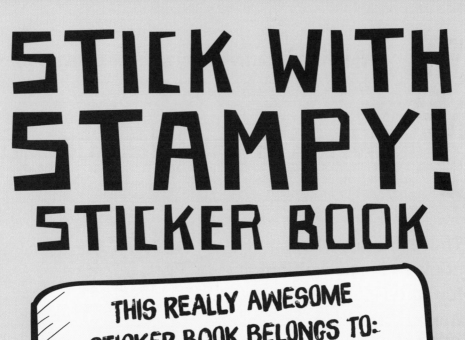

THIS REALLY AWESOME
STICKER BOOK BELONGS TO:

Ryan

EGMONT
We bring stories to life

First published in Great Britain in 2016 by Egmont UK Limited,
The Yellow Building, 1 Nicholas Road, London, W11 4AN

Illustrations by Army of Trolls and Anthony Duke.
Edited by Mara Alperin.
Designed by Anthony Duke.
Consultant: Marco Kahlhamer.

ISBN 978 1 4052 8421 9
64601/1
Printed in Italy

Adult supervision is recommended when glue, paint, scissors and sharp points are in use.

ONLINE SAFETY FOR YOUNGER FANS
Spending time online is great fun!
Here are a few simple rules to help younger fans stay safe and keep
the internet a great place to spend time:

• Never give out your real name – don't use it as your username.
• Never give out any of your personal details.
• Never tell anybody which school you go to or how old you are.
• Never tell anybody your password except a parent or a guardian.
• Be aware that you must be 13 or over to create an account on many sites.
• Always check the site policy and ask a parent or guardian for permission before registering.
• Always tell a parent or guardian if something is worrying you.

IT'S STICKER TIME!

WELCOME to my lovely sticker book. I can't wait to get started!

What's inside for you:

There are lots of cool stickers inside waiting for you. You can use them in this book, or **CREATE YOUR OWN SCENES!**

SUPER STICKERS

PUZZLES AND GAMES

This book is packed with activities, cool game ideas and more. **IT'S HOURS OF FUN!**

LETTERS, A FLIP BOOK, A ONE-OF-A-KIND BOARD GAME ... AND LOTS MORE! Plus, two giant posters of **ME** and my friends.

MEET MY FRIENDS!

Meet **iBALLiSTiCSQUiD, SQAiSHEY** and **AMY LEE**. They are my best friends online and in real life.

FIND THE STICKER!
Sometimes my friends like to say silly things! Can you match them to their catchphrases?

Poop Attack!

meanie beanies!

LOVES IT!

Fun Fact
SQAiSHEY GOT HER NAME FROM A NICKNAME SHE HAD FOR HER PET HAMSTER!

Fun Fact
SQUiD HAS LOTS OF PETS INCLUDING CATS, DOGS, TARANTULAS AND CHICKENS!

Fun Fact
AMY LEE USED TO BE A FAN OF MY VIDEOS BEFORE WE BECAME FRIENDS!

The answers are on page 18.

MY SPACE MISSION

Today I'm going to go into outer space. But **WAIT!** First we need to fly there. Use the stickers to build a space craft for me!

My space craft
is called: _____

What should I pack with me?
Choose as many as you like!

Toothbrush ☐
Star map ☐
Warm jumper ☐
Sunglasses ☐
Camera ☐
Trumpet ☐

Journal ☐
Cake ☐
Roller skates ☐
Rubber ducks ☐
Flowers ☐
Pizza ☐

How do you organise a party in outer space?

You PLANET! He! He! He!

Fun Fact

DID YOU KNOW A ROCKET SHIP CAN FLY AT ALMOST 25,000 MILES PER HOUR?

5

PLANET STAMPY

A whole **NEW PLANET!** Use stickers and doodles to complete this amazing new world.

AHHHH! WHAT'S THIS SCARY THING?

6

DRAW A SILLY
SPACE ALIEN
HERE!

Add somewhere I can sleep. ZZZZZZz

What do you call an alien with six eyes?

An aliiiiiien! He! He! He!

THIS TAKES THE CAKE

MMM ... what a tasty-looking cake! Add some stickers to decorate it.

Who are you going to share it with?

(PICK ME!)

(PICK ME!)

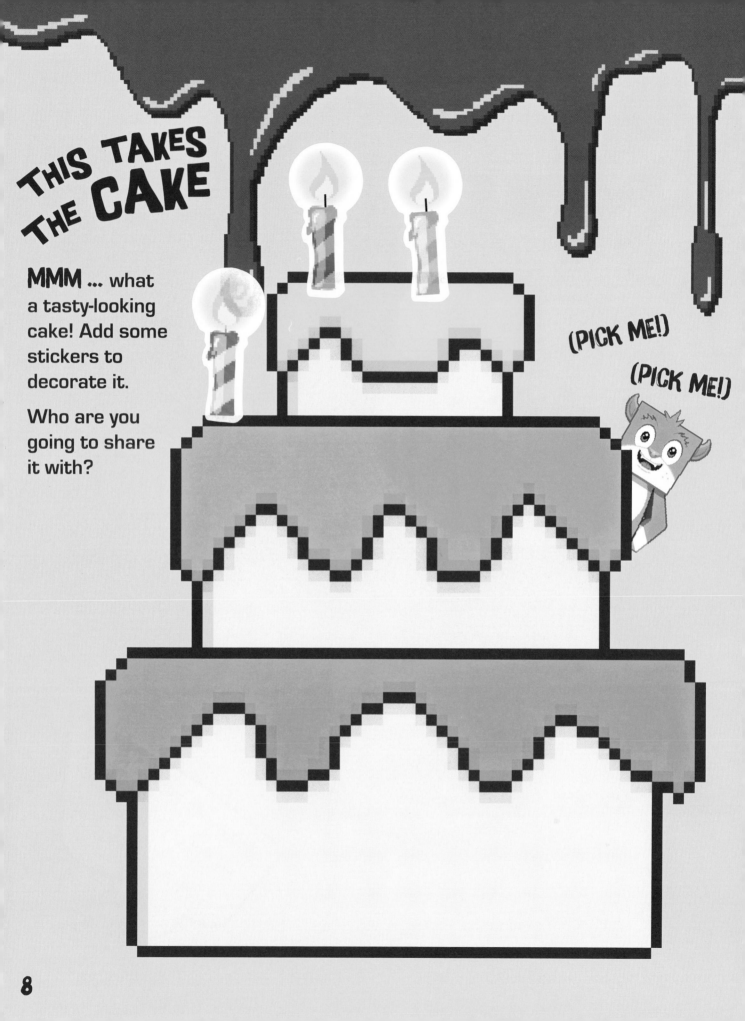

8

MY FAVOURITE THINGS

CAKE is **MY FAVOURITE** thing! Can you match my friends to a sticker of their favourite thing?

 LOVES

 LOVES

 LOVES

WHAT DO YOU LIKE?

MY FAVOURITE THINGS ARE: ....

AND ....,

BUT DEFINITELY **NOT** ....!

The answers are on page 18.

SQUID'S SEARCH & FIND

I'm on an **OCEAN ADVENTURE** with **SQUID.** Help Squid find all his treasure!

STAMPY:02

Add a sticker when you find each hidden object.

Did you hear about the skunk that fell into a lake and stank to the bottom? Tee Hee!

CAN YOU BEAT STAMPY?

WOW, these are some tough trivia questions! Here are my answers, BUT can you get more right than I did? Write in your guesses below, and then check the answers on page 18.

1 True or false: Slugs use their tentacles to smell.

Your answer:

....

Stampy says:

FALSE
....

2 True or false: A crocodile cannot stick his tongue out.

Your answer:

....

Stampy says:

TRUE
....

3 Which animal has the largest eyes in the world?

Your answer:

....

Stampy says:

GIANT
SQUID
....

4 What was the first animal sent into outer space?

Your answer:

....

Stampy says:

A
DOG
....

 Did you beat Stampy?

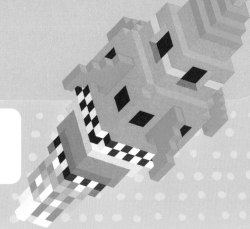

The answers are on page 18.

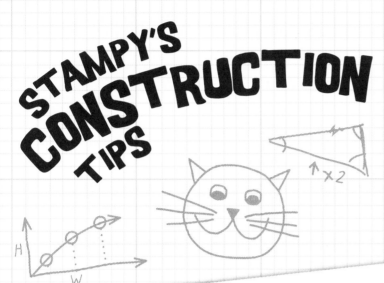

STAMPY'S CONSTRUCTION TIPS

You have an **IDEA** for something you want to build so now you need to **PLAN IT**.

Tips:
○ Sketch what you want to build below.
○ Gather all of the materials you need.
○ Build it!
○ Make small tweaks to improve it.
○ Admire your work!

THIS IS MY PLAN TO BUILD: diagon alley

MATERIALS NEEDED: Stone, Redwool, glassPane, Sign, Wood, stairs, fence, door, stick, bricks, sandstone,

iBALLISTIC
SQUID   STAMPY

SQAISHEY

AMY LEE

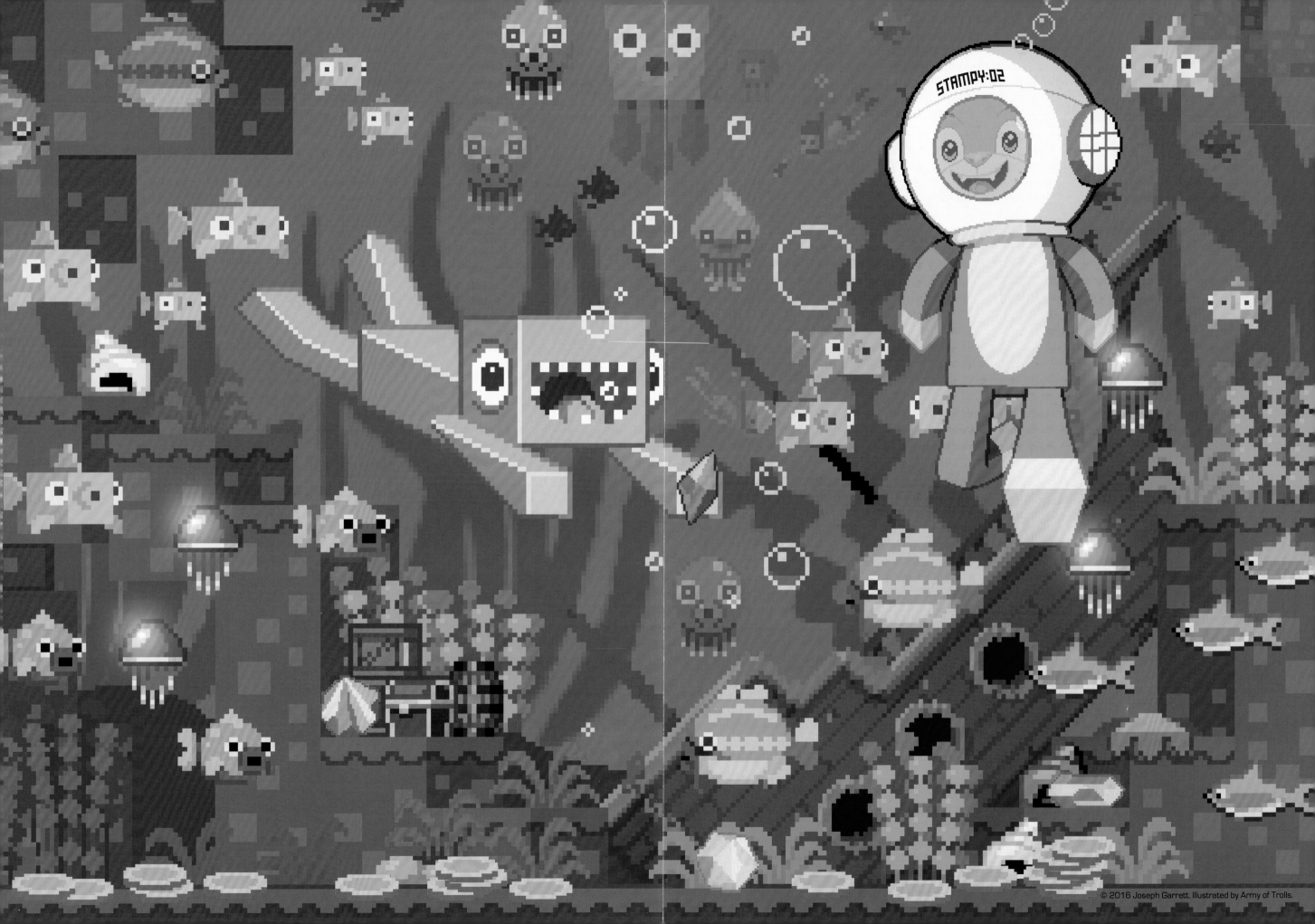

DON'T FORGET TO WRITE!

When I go on **QUESTS**, I like to keep my friends updated. Why not send a **LETTER?**

Cut out the letter below, and follow the instructions on page 14 to fold it into an envelope.

DON'T FORGET TO PUT THE CORRECT ADDRESS!

POST OFFICE

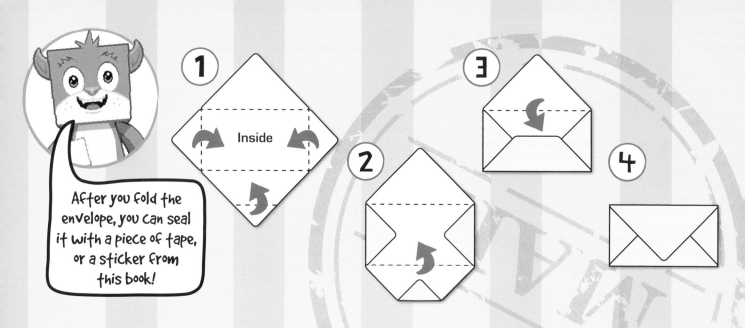

1 Inside

2

3

4

After you fold the envelope, you can seal it with a piece of tape, or a sticker from this book!

HELLO

FROM

14

STAMPY'S LOVELY CAKES

MMM ... look at those **TASTY CAKES!** Cut the pieces out and follow the directions on the back. **TA-DA!** You'll have two scrumptious cakes.

Fun Fact

THE LARGEST CUPCAKE EVER MADE WAS OVER 1 METRE TALL AND OVER 3 METRES WIDE. WOW!

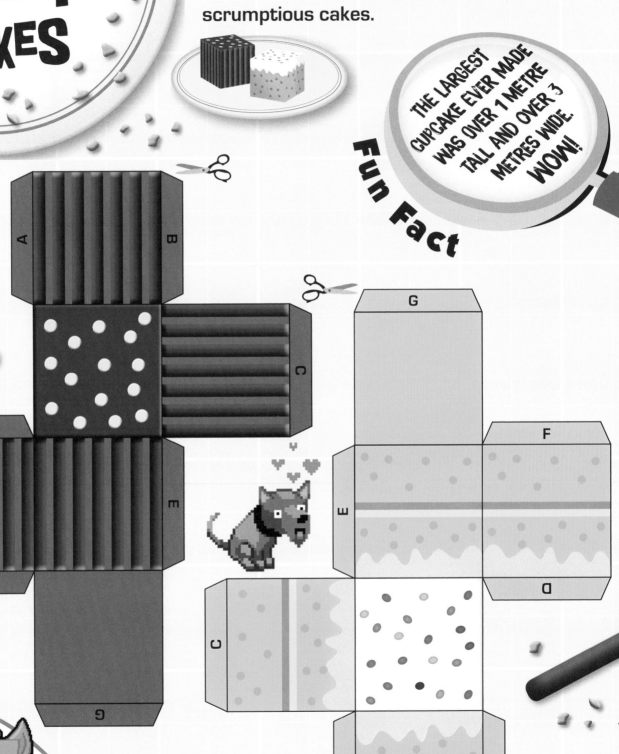

Save some for me!

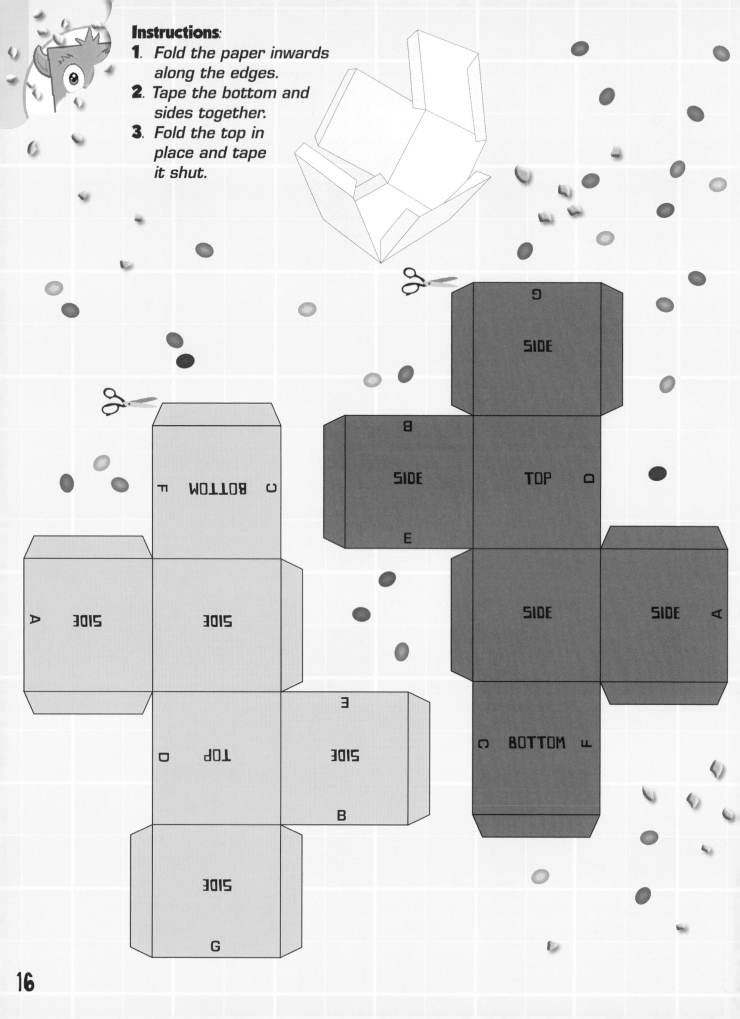

Instructions:
1. Fold the paper inwards along the edges.
2. Tape the bottom and sides together.
3. Fold the top in place and tape it shut.

SIDE G

SIDE B

SIDE E

TOP D

SIDE

SIDE A

BOTTOM C F

BOTTOM F C

TOP D

SIDE E

SIDE B

SIDE

SIDE A

SIDE G

FINGER PUPPETS

OOH, these are some lovely FINGER PUPPETS. You can use the finger puppets to perform a show or even to make your own video!

1. Cut out the finger puppets and colour them in.

2. Glue or tape each puppet so it fits around your finger.

3. Don't forget to give each puppet a different voice!

Stampy's tips:

1. When performing a show or making a video, it might help to have a basic plan or script, but don't be afraid to improvise!

2. Be creative! You can act out a story you know, or make up something new.

3. Try using the pull-out poster of Stampy's Theatre for a backdrop to your show!

Answers: Page 3: Squid - Poop Attack!; Sqaishey - Meanie Beanies!; Amy Lee - Loves it!
Page 9: Squid - party hat, Amy Lee - red rose, Sqaishey - pumpkin pie.
Page 11: true, true, giant squid, a dog.

FLIP BOOK

Make your own FLIP BOOK and watch me eat my cake – YUM!

1. Cut out all the pages of the flip book.
2. Put the pages in order, from 1 to 12.
3. Clip the pages together with a bulldog clip.
4. Flip the pages with your thumb to see what happens.

BONUS
if you flip the book upside-down, you'll have another flip book of Sqaishey trying to fly!

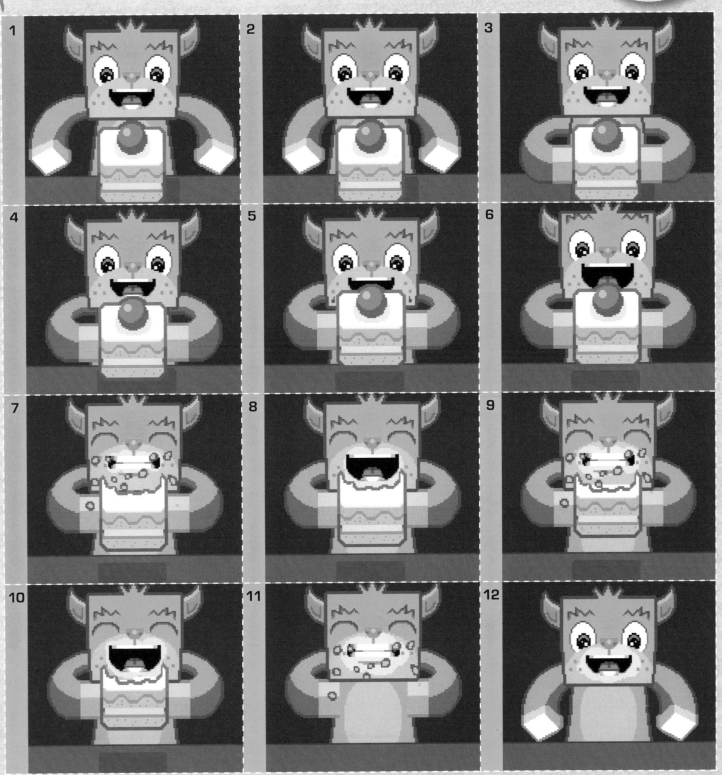

19

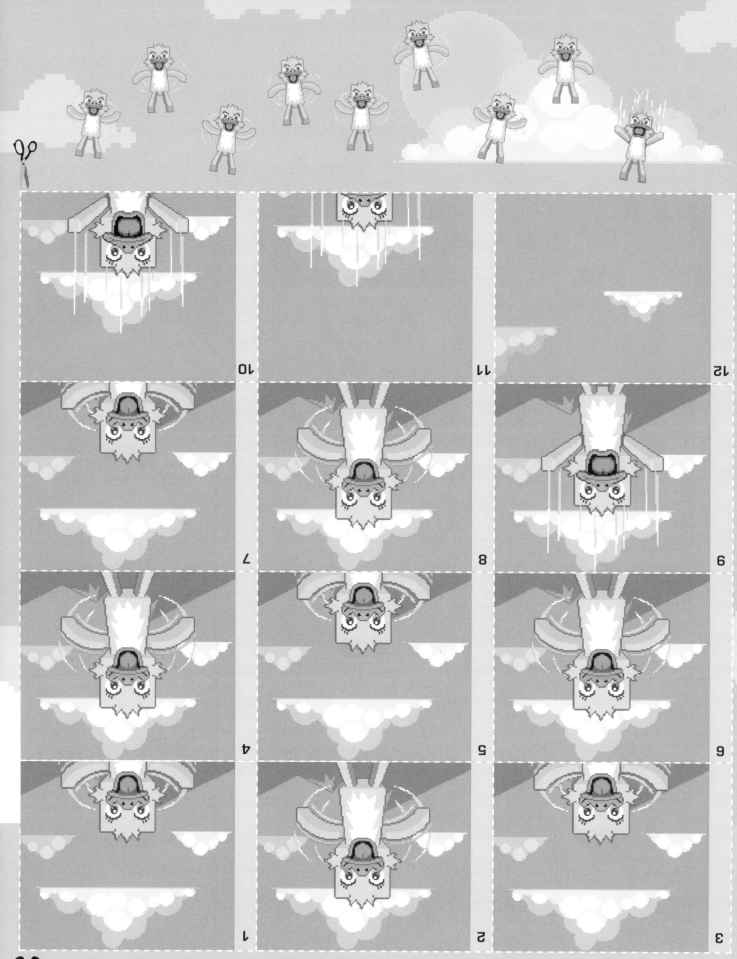

20

FRIENDS QUIZ

HERE'S A CHALLENGE! How well do you know your friends? Take this fun quiz to find out.

*Cut out the two answer cards. Ask an adult if you need help. You and your friend each fill out your own answer card. **No peeking!** Then guess each other's answers. You get one point for each correct answer. I've put down my answers as well!*

Question ?	Your answer	Guess what your friend will say	What Stampy says
1 What pizza toppings would your friend choose?			Chicken and BBQ sauce.
2 If they could play any instrument, what would it be?			Accordion.
3 What's their favourite way to eat a potato?			With baked beans.
4 If they could wake up with a super power, what would it be?			To be able to control time.
5 Would they prefer to live in: a mountain cabin, a beach house, or a giant castle?			Giant castle.

Question ?	Your answer	Guess what your friend will say	What Stampy says
1 What pizza toppings would your friend choose?			Chicken and BBQ sauce.
2 If they could play any instrument, what would it be?			Accordion.
3 What's their favourite way to eat a potato?			With baked beans.
4 If they could wake up with a super power, what would it be?			To be able to control time.
5 Would they prefer to live in: a mountain cabin, a beach house, or a giant castle?			Giant castle.

Invisibility

Drums

Eat as much
chocolate as
I want

Banana
and beetroot

A mountain
cabin

A beach house

Banjo

Talk to animals

In my pyjamas

Sausage
and onion

Guitar

With chocolate
sprinkles on top

Standing on my head

With salt
and vinegar

Mashed with
cheese

Strawberries
and onion

Clarinet

A giant castle

I'd like to fly

One at a time

Coconut
and fried egg

Ukulele

Breathe
underwater

See with my
eyes closed

Rhubarb
and lemon

With a fork

Piano

STAMPY'S BOARD GAME

Want to create your own **SPECIAL BOARD GAME?** Well, you've come to the right place!

Before you play ...

Use the hexagon stickers in this book to create your own,

ONE-OF-A-KIND BOARD GAME!

Add each rule wherever you like, or make your own new rules. Don't forget to pick a **SILLY WORD** *to* **SHOUT** *at the end.*

How to play ...

1. *Use buttons or coins as pieces. Place your pieces on START and take turns rolling the dice to move.*

2. *Move forwards the number of squares shown on the dice, then follow the instructions on each space.*

3. *The first person to reach the end* **IS THE WINNER!**